MW00652663

"When the Divine Speaks, the Heart Listens"

By Reina Hallab

Volume I

♥

When The Divine Speaks, The Heart Listens

ISBN: 978-1-7781486-0-6
ISBN eBook: 978-1-7781486-2-0
Publisher Raw Healing Love
Book designed by Reina Hallab
Edited by Heidi Marie Klein

♥

To my parents Zeina and Refaat, I am forever thankful for the love you seeded within me in this lifetime, for enduring all my ups and downs, the challenges and the shifts. And for finally accepting my path of deep connection. Mom, Dad, I Love you.

To my siblings Nora and Mohamad-Riad, who are with me all the way. Thank you for believing in me. I Love you dearly.

To my grandmothers Fatima and Yemen, you taught me love and generosity as well as resilience, strength, and empowerment. I am truly blessed.

To my nephew Rafi, since your birth, watching you grow year after year has taught me the true meaning of unconditional love and kindness, and how to be a fearless and an adventurous soul.
My Love forever.

To my niece Mia, observing the empowerment you hold within from the moment you were born, and the way you affirm your presence, along with simply being you, have encouraged me to be me. You are my sweet young lady, and I Love you forever more.

My Invitation to my beloved readers

I encourage you to read with your heart, and allow the energy of truth, love, kindness and compassion, to take you on a soulful journey with me and guide you to elevate your spirit within.

Please take a few deep, conscious, and mindful breaths all the way through your reading in order to grasp all that is present for you at this moment.

With all my love, respect, and peace to you
In-Joy this Treat!

Reina

BREATHE

"Our Breath is a Gift,
it is the Present,
in the Here and NOW"

TABLE OF CONTENTS

INFINITE DIVINE LOVE

FOREWORD

Reina Hallab is a very special person, some kind of exceptional guru, an angel able to delicately, suavely and divinely enter your heart, your soul and cleanse them in order to reveal a better you, a true you, the one that was hiding within you for so long.

Reina takes you on an unforgettable tour to discover the angels and demons, the heaven and hell that dwell deep within you.

She'll gently guide you through everything that has happened in your life until you come across that one thing, that one event or that one person that moved you deeply and changed your life.

You'll feel so good, so liberated, so trusting that you will gladly open the door that will allow her into the mysteries and secrets hidden deep within you.

And, without any warning, sudden and liberating tears will start rolling down your cheeks.

Thanks to her soothing, refreshing and reassuring voice, you finally found your true you.

You've just arrived, you've just come home, you've just found your other self.

You feel as if a suffocating, heavy weight has just been lifted off your shoulders.

This is Reina's miraculous potion.

And she calls it Raw Healing.

Once you've tasted it, you'll shake and cry like you never shook and cried before.

You'll feel so happy, so light and so free because you just realized that the evil that took possession of your inner being for so long has finally been discovered and vanquished.

Rachid Amokrane
President of Smarttek Consulting Inc

PREFACE

This book is a generous collection of inspirational and motivational quotes that my higher spirit and divine forces graciously bequeathed upon me. Along with short anecdotes of my life, which lead me to live this enlightening peaceful path.

We all have a story to share. Mine is for you to witness that "everything is possible".

Have you encountered, while sleeping peacefully, being awakened by an energy leading you to do something just like that?

Well. I have.

This divine energy has been visiting me, guiding me, and waking me up to write, since 2011.

This time, on the 2nd of July, 2021, I was ushered, at 8 am, towards my computer to compile a book I have always dreamed of writing.

The first manuscript was ready, even designed.
I have also reached out to all the big conscious publishing houses, emailing and calling.
And no reply. So I procrastinated a whole year.

Since life works in mysterious ways, on March 1st, 2022, I was invited on a tour to Africa, Niamey capital of Niger, to join one of the top public speakers and personal development coaches as a collaborator and business partner.

I accepted, joined the stage, and witnessed lots of hands on life transformation stories.

I was in an awe.

I was told: "You have a 'GIFT' the whole world needs to learn about, get ready to share this gift, with an adjoin book"

Let's fast rewind first to April the 18th, 2016. I asked my dear friend Sylvain Bergeron to volunteer at one of the big Public Speaking conferences he was organizing in Montreal, Canada. He accepted and requested me to accompany one of the top speakers during his stay.

I did, without knowing who that gentlemen was.

I am a very transparent person, just like an open book, and during our drive from the airport to the hotel and over some drinks at the hotel bar, I shared my story along with my writings.

He was very impressed to the point he encouraged me to prepare an anthology of my collection. He said: "I will help you edit, print and publish. you have 6 months.

I took all that in. And the following day, I attended the conference.

I was amazed by the energy, the subject, the enthusiasm he was radiating. He was introduced as a Leadership Advisor, NLP and personal development coach, Speaker, and Author, that was Dr. Rachid Amokrane.

Following what I have witnessed, and being motivated by a well-known coach, believe it or not, I thought I was too small to make such a big jump, so I froze.

Fast forward to 2021, I made it happen.

Following our tour in Africa, he advised me to have the book ready. He said: “The doors of Africa, & Asia will be open for you. Be Present.”

I am so grateful to Dr. Amokrane for believing in me, guiding me, and showing me the way. You are one of my intangible forces on this earth.
I am forever thankful.

PART I
Introduction

This is an inspirational book, dedicated to anyone who feels a touch of love by the divine, within and around.

May this book motivates you to discover the hidden seeds within you, that need to be nourished, loved, cared for and embodied.

Remember, this grain is slowly seedling into becoming a tree that is thriving to be seen. She is ready to flourish and blossom. Allow it to be perceived.

Eventually, the True Self is what we are seeking, she is engraved within us and fully "PRESENT" in the here and now.

She is our "GIFT of LIFE" and only needs to be awakened.

INNER TRUTH

"Dwell in every moment
& Awaken your soul within
So you always Express Fully,
your inner Truth"

UNITE & DWELL WITHIN

As I write in this moment, I feel the words flowing through my breath, my heart, into my fingers. My whole body is shivering!

I look through my window and witness two crows flying almost "wing in wing".

What a perfect image of "UNITY", even in the light of darkness.

COMMUNICATION

"Communication
is the basic recipe of a relation,
if it doesn't exist,
the rest will fade away"

PART II
The Journey

MY JOURNEY "INTO BEING"

My journey "into being" started when I was born.

Sounds were heard through my inner ear, and I never understood.

Growing up, I drew on my school notebooks, many shapes and lines, many signatures and hearts, and always one eye.

The voice kept on speaking louder and louder, faster and faster, until my hands couldn't carry.

So I stopped.

OPPORTUNITIES

"Good Moments and Opportunities in life, don't last long.

If you feel it, see it, and even touch it,
just grab it with your arms,
hold it tight, give it all the emotions
and love, and just go for it...

as once gone, there is no way back...
and one day you don't want to wake up
regretting...

because you have been busy with other
life problems"

THE SEEDS OF MY INNER TRANSFORMATION

It was in a moment of slow awakening that it all came back to me, in those times when I never thought I could ever "CONNECT".

A rush of emotions flowed in me mysteriously.
I, myself, was even in awe.

It all started in 1997 when "The Seeds of My Inner Transformation" were planted. I was only 16.

Fascinated by Numerology*, the pseudo-scientific belief in a divine mystical relationship between a number and coinciding events.
I connect with the number 16**.

1 plus 6 is equal to the number 7 & 1997 to the number 8. Linking the 7th*** into the 8th.

From "VICTORY" into the "INFINITE"

*Numerology Ref: https://artsandculture.google.com/entity/numerology/
**16: The numerology number 16 is a philosopher with sound arguments. It tends to look for and find answers within, from a well of contemporary and ancient wisdom. Ref: affinitynumerology.com
***7th in Arabic has the shape of a V. V as in Victory. And 8, horizontally, becomes the infinite sign.

RELATIONSHIP

“A Relationship is simply
a pure friendship,
mixed with tingling emotions,
sprinkled with lots of passion
and cooked with Love”

LETTING GO & ACCEPTING

The "UNITY"* is always present**, even in the darkest times.

I remember, it all happened during the 'blurry moments' on May 7th, 1997***, the time I underwent my first nine hours brain aneurysm surgery. This is where, my inner light shined, and I intertwined with the Infinite Divine.

My readiness to "LET GO" is what saved me.

Releasing all life's expectations and attachments, to whether, positive or negative likelihood of, surviving or dying, missing any physical movement, sight or hearing, allowed my awareness to expand into the "PRESENT".

Trust me, being in what we call, "The Present Moment" was not something I was familiar with. It was one that I have experienced conscientiously.

Fear simply stopped from existing. "ACCEPTANCE" was my power and then, only "LOVE" flowed.

* Unity is the alignment with the "Divine, God, the Infinite self, the universe"
**Present: defined as a GIFT of Life
***May 7th 1997--> numerology = 11 Master Number

! EXPECTATIONS

"Expectations joggle your dreams,
erase the surprises,
and can make your life miserable.

Life has a lot to offer

let it be unpredictable

so you can maximize the enjoyments"

REBIRTH

It was following the second, seven-week surgery*, which coincidentally fell on the same date I was born, is where I sensed a new birth, May 20th, 1997. My 17th Birthday.

My numerological description of being "REBORN"* into the "INFINITE"**, is about letting go of the ego into the spirit. What an incredible rebirth.

This was my aha moment, nothing I ever imagined would happen.

"GRATITUDE" was and still is the "MAGICAL" word of all, "الحمدلله", Al Hamdou Li Allah.

Always good to remember:

The "MAGIC" is all around us, all we need is to "LISTEN"

*the Surgery was an Angiography. An angiogram is a test that takes X-ray pictures of the coronary arteries and the vessels that supply blood to the heart. During an angiogram, a special dye is released into the coronary arteries from a catheter (special tube) inserted in a blood vessel.
Ref:https://www.heartandstroke.ca/heart-disease/tests/angiography
**REBORN: May 20, 1997 = 33 -> The Jesus Year is age 33, the year that scholars believe Jesus started a spiritual, political, and intellectual revolution & his traditional age when he was crucified and resurrected.
My translation to Letting go of the ego into the spirit. According to Al-Ghazali the dwellers of Heaven will exist eternally in a state of being at age 33.
Ref: https://en.wikipedia.org/wiki/33_(number)
**The number 33, when it mirrors the number becomes 8, and 1+7=8, the INFINITE

YOUR TRUE GUIDE

"Thy Soul is your true guide, your multiple senses to receive & perceive information.

Be in its awareness & listen, as it is your only key to your true self, & your true path.

Messengers, synchronicities and signs come your way in reality, dreams & other forms to confirm every information.

Be in its grace, its gratitude, & love it, as it oversees & protects you from what ever is not serving you in this lifetime."

I BELIEVE IN MYSELF

Magic was fully present right after that day in some ways.

It shows itself, then hides.

Believing in my "Self" created more enchantment, significantly when no one believed in me.

It was the following year when I went back to school; Grade 12. I chose to proceed with two years in one, against all the wishes of my professors and classmates.

I thrived, succeeded, and surprised my surroundings, and within me, I said,

"I know 'I CAN'"

"I BELIEVE in MYSELF"

BELIEVE IN YOURSEFL

" NEVER GET DISCOURAGED BY THE OPINIONS OF OTHERS

BELIEVE IN YOURSELF

THE POWERS YOU HAVE, AND WITH YOUR PERSISTENCE,

YOU WILL HIGHLY ACHIEVE.
ONLY YOU WILL KNOW,

WITH THE PASSION YOU HAVE,
NOTHING IS UNACHIEVABLE "

LIFE HAPPENS

Then, "Life Happened".

Without really understanding the deeper meaning of life, and like every human living in this society, we always forget to live genuinely.

We dive into the missions of the planned limited existence, and we lose ourselves in this chaos.

Until something hits back, and we "AWAKE"*

I did.

* awake, many people go through suffering, be it a sickness, an accident, a loss of someone dear, a job, material stuff, etc...

BLESSED

“Being blessed, is to have awaken to witness a new decade uncover
Being blessed, is to wake up breathing life
Being blessed, is knowing even in the days you feel lonely, you are never alone
Being blessed, is to witness a shift and transformation in life where people are coming together in love & gratitude
Being blessed, is simply thanking the life you have, and feeling it in depth of your heart
Being blessed, is knowing that what you have is beyond material, it is your soul connection, & connection to every soul in your life & beyond.

Always Being blessed with the health & perseverance to simply live in humbleness and be present to serve

A simple full love gratitude to be, in this lifetime, still alive, breathing & healthy!

It only takes a Thank You!

THE MIRACULOUS MIXTURE

The miraculous mixture of, the TRUE meaning of my birth name, the shift to raw living food and the healing energy initiation, was the blossoming "PRESENTS" of my "AWAKENING".

A new Shift in my being took place, as if the Seeds of My Inner Transformation, and after 14 years, started seedling.

The plant grew with more awareness, and the "SELF-DISCOVERY JOURNEY" began.

LOVE RECIPES

"Life, is a delicious meal,
prepared with organic ingredients, wrapped with love, and sent to you from the universe.

Before you open to taste, make sure to read the label.

It contains:
Pure love, freedom of being, respect to self, self-love, self-appreciation, worthiness, lots of happiness, full of positive moments, incredible synchronicities, and a strong intuition.

Make sure your label of life says the same, otherwise change it to BE IT!

Life is your present, live it truly and fully.
With my love to you!"

MY TRUE NAME

The soul always chooses the family she would like to be born into; mine did.

They named me Rena. Then, I added the "I"*.

It happened when I started writing my name at school, I was seven years old.

Rena felt too masculine, and the "I" filled the balance.

In May 2010, I felt the urge to look up the true meaning of my name, RENA**, that was following my nephew's birth and name search, to realize that it actually means "REBORN"

I was grateful - the message was received.

*RENA-->REINA
**https://www.thenamemeaning.com/rena/

BIRTH

"My eyes are drawing you,
I'm inhaling your smell,
tasting your charm &
challenging your thoughts,
you are within me...

It is time to be born"

THE SHIFT

When "RAW" came into my life in 2009, the timing was spot on. It was the year I discovered, following countless regular MRI* check-ups, that I have a meningioma**. A benign tumor in the right side of my frontal lobe.

Imagine, twelve years ago, I had the left side of my brain open, in addition to undergoing a full week of cerebral angiographies, without being fully sedated, to block a main artery in my brain. I surely wasn't ready for another head surgery, and definitely not ready now.

With my natural way of living, healthy lifestyle, and positive way of being, I managed to help stabilize the tumor, and performing toward releasing it fully from my physical body and energy. Let's pray for the healing to present itself.

*MRI A magnetic resonance imaging
**A meningioma is a primary central nervous system (CNS) tumor. This means it begins in the brain or spinal cord - Ref: https://www.cancer.gov/rare-brain-spine-tumor/tumors/meningioma

THE MIND

“ The mind is a manipulator, always builds a block against the heart so only the mind speaks.

Heart murmurs are transparent and pure; they drive your instinct on the path to feel and acknowledge the true action.

Let it be free, listen and dive in ”

"LET FOOD BE THY MEDICINE AND MEDICINE BE THY FOOD". —HIPPOCRATES.

Raw Living Food brought me back to life.

The discovery, the energy, and the connection got stronger every second.

My "INNER LISTENING" skills grew, and my Raw Love Recipes blog was born on March 1st, 2012.

"Raw - because it is pure from my heart, thoughts, and mind.

Love - because I believe it is around in all life elements, and

Recipes - because I create them by adding my own ingredients."

FREEDOM

“ The freedom of being alive

Living in happiness without limitations, opening up to this universe to create all the beauties in your life for you.

Gratitude is what makes it happen

Glow in your spirit, believe in your soul, follow your intuition, most of all,
Just BE! ”

UNCOVER THE DIAMOND OF SELF-LOVE

My journey was my own challenge to uncover the diamond within.

I choose to make a difference to heal myself and live a "dis-ease free" life.

Since that mind shift, sickness left, and discovering "SELF-LOVE" was on the horizon. It was too far to be seen, touched, or felt until all came into place and the deeper connection with the Divine blossomed.

This became my mantra:

"LIFE, SHOW ME YOUR MAGIC"™

SELFLESS

Love was well-defined in life, or at least we thought it was, until self-love bestowed itself in its strangest moments.

I couldn't even utter the sentence, not even write: "I LOVE REINA". The process was painful.

During my Energy Healing Master Level with my Mother, the connection to the womb I was born into was present to hold, love, support, and witness me as the butterfly, freeing itself from the word selfish into "SELFLESS, " was born.

EGO VS LOVE

“Sailing in the present moment on the
rhythm of love, powers to create
wonders & magic.

Expectation found its way in
& managed to drill holes allowing
misery to come in.

The boat started sinking, it couldn't sail
with expectations & misery.
Its only wind was flowing within the
energy of love, moments and creations.

Choosing to save the ego first leaving
Love behind to drown, was selfish

Luckily & through the balancing waves,
the strong current & wind,
Love found its way back to the shore to
embrace life again, open its arms to
anything that comes its way.
Remember, Love overpowers ego.”

SEEDS OF LOVE

And the journey continues, as nothing stops from manifesting. The process is ongoing. And every moment, we strive to "THRIVE."

As my 'Inner Listening' grew, my 'Inner' plant continued blooming, so I rose into a well-grounded, fearless, mighty tree whose branches expanded and flourished with fruits.

Here, I share my fruits and all its source to plant a seed of "LOVE" in your heart. My path of service paved its road for guiding all beings who cross my path into discovering their own "TRUTH."

SAVIOUR

“We only know the depth of our soul

when we bow in gratefulness to the
magnifying power that created it

Look deeply into your eyes to touch a
drop of its beauty

For whenever you feel lost or scared

always know, how deep in you is your
saviour

Trust this life that runs through your
veins & flourish with its majestic love”

ASK & YOU SHALL RECEIVE

The "CREATOR", the "LOVER", the "DIVINE LIGHT", "GOD"
communicates with me in heavenly nature

Words I can hear
Images I can see
Messages I receive
Surprises, I simply bow in "ADMIRATION."

How marvelous to "ASK" and always "RECEIVE."
I have a "SOUL" that hears, sees, feels, blossoms, and LOVES

I am not special, "WE ALL ARE"

TRANSFORMATIONAL LESSONS

"We all pass through different moments every day, & the beauty of it, is that they are all our perfect teachers.
They come as a present, to shape us, to ground us, to elevate us & help us grow, whether it's an emotional pain, vulnerability, loneliness, & weaknesses, and/or, an emotional gain, happiness, joyfulness & passion.

Embrace every moment, even when it is so hard to welcome
learn from it, let it vibrate in our cells, to awaken us, give us strengths, & remind us of our true selves.

Remember, there will always be a sign, a message or messengers which will come our way to guide us, open our eyes, heart, & soul & bring us back to our aligned self.

Let the magic do its work through welcoming every moment in love & gratitude, & remember to always follow our intuitive side, as it always shows us the way to heaven."

DIVINE LOVE WITHIN

My Conversations with the "SOURCE ENERGY" were sowing the seeds to guide me into Loving my Self as a start.

I never knew, cultivating the "DIVINE LOVE WITHIN", was ultimately much more profound.

When I feel this "LOVE," my inner euphoria, happiness & tears overflow as I become "ONE" with "GOD."

My "HEART" expands and just wants to "EMBRACE" all BEINGS, to touch a sense of its drops - 'ahhhh.'

"TOGETHERNESS IS ONENESS"

“ Powerful energies grow

when

togetherness becomes oneness!

May the power of being

reach you

elevate you

and

always nourish you! ”

SELF-DISCOVERY

A big part of my embarked Journey with Self-Discovery was with writing inspirational quotes*.

And I share:

"It touches deeply my soul every time I type, starting from the first word to the end. I get this emotional, tangible feeling, an internal warmth aiding my fingers to play around, touching every letter with deep sentiments.

I have never thought that one day I will be able to calligraphically project this burst of emotion, passion, and love into words, a phrase, or even a quote."
Nonetheless,

"A BOOK."

*The writing began at the start of my journey, on December 14. 2011 - It has been 11 years.
MASTER NUMBER 11: The Master Intuitive. It is a dreamer. Master number 11 has all the aspects of the 2, but is considerably enhanced and charged with charisma, leadership, and inspiration. ref: https://www.worldnumerology.com/numerology-master-numbers/master-number-11/

SEEDS

"Planting the seeds at the start

in a comfortable relation

nourishing it daily

will harvest a wonderful loving
life"

LOVE IS A SEED

English, was my first insight into the birth of my writings, then I dwelled into French, followed by Arabic, which is my native language.

Only that, I haven't written Arabic literature for over 2 decades.

When the words are an inspiration from the Divine, the voice is heard, in all languages, and the Heart simply listens, and mine did indeed.

The word 'Love' in Arabic is 'حُب' {Hob}, and using some accentuation, the word itself changes & 'حَب' {Hab} means 'Seeds'.

For me, This is POWERFUL

PLANTING THE SEEDS

"Inspiration is my world

Motivation is what I strive for

Planting the seeds within you is what I'll teach you

Believing in your powers is my way to serve you

Living the magical life is what I thrive for

Come along with me

& I'll show you the way"

LET IT BE NOW, FOREVER!

My journey into being started when I was born.

And I am grateful to have followed my intuition and connected deeper to the CREATOR, "THE LOVER, THE DIVINE, THE SOURCE ENERGY, THE UNIVERSE, GOD, ALLĀH, ٱللَّٰه."

"I AM ALWAYS LISTENING, WRITING & SHARING YOUR WISDOM TO MANIFEST INTO CREATION"

LET IT BE - NOW FOREVER

PART III
The Inspirations

INSPIRATIONAL FREE SPIRIT QUOTES

Here I am sharing my inspiration from the Divine.

In all Languages.

May your energy bathe in the spirit of

Divine Love, Omnipresence, & Omnipotent Words.

I am inviting you to receive this touch of Love.

In-Joy
Sincerely Yours
Reina - Free Spirit, روحٌ حرّة

☮ المُسْتَسْلِمُ لِلسَلام

"المُسلِمُ المُسَالِمُ، مسَلِّمُ السَلام"

SURRENDERER TO PEACE 

"*The Peaceful Surrenderer,*
Surrenders to Peace"

الكريمِ

"كَرَمُ الكريمِ، من ما كَرَّم به الكريمُ

فالكَرَمُ من كَرمِ الجميع

أكرِم نفَسَك من ما كرِّمتَ به

لتُكرِم لك الدنيا من ملذاتِ كَرَمِها"

THE GENEROUS

“The generously bountiful is inherited from the generosity of the Divine Abundance

This munificent plentifulness is the generosity of all beings

Lavish yourself with the infinite abundance

And life will generously offer you all its richness”

FORGIVENESS

"FORGIVENESS IS A GIFT, MASTER IT TO SET YOU FREE"

As I observe the beings I gave birth to

A breath of "MY SELF"

Are in a bubble of darkness, wandering around chasing an unsolved matter within them

Actually, it is what is being projected outside of them

All the fear, the worry, the sickness & the death...

They don't believe that their soul never dies

For people, who are worried to let go of the material, how can they connect to the deepest of what I have given them?

"The breath of an "ADVENTUROUS SOUL,"

which flies around and is sent on this earth to manifest their role, their mission of awakening each other, in "COMPASSION", "KINDNESS" and "GENEROSITY"

Are they first ready for "FORGIVENESS" so they can "MANIFEST" it all?

Who is ready to forgive?

As I am a "FORGIVER," how can they not be!"

Signed by GOD

 WHEN THE DIVINE SPEAKS

The unspoken can not be spoken
It is only felt

As I master you, I perfect you, you become all that is, and you manifest my creation...

I speak through you, so you guide all others
To believe in creation and to follow their intuition
Only that, will illuminate them from their narrow mindedness
So they expand and feel my creation.

Do you believe the people are ready to see the light I drew for them toward their destiny?
Or they are afraid of the power I gave them
So they are still acting small...

Only when they feel that beat in their heart, that shivers in their being, & surely their blush in their whole self, then they will feel my existence, in all, especially in them.
The human, the animals, the nature, the planets, and the galaxies. I'm here to enlighten them, so they live in the heaven on earth I created for them.

Signed by GOD

CREATION

“ Creation is all that we are

We think that we think

though we simply observe

Instantly

we intuit

so we create what we feel

& it blossomly manifests

Positively or negatively

Again

a simple choice

Wise is the being

Intelligence is a consideration

Enigma, our mysterious creation ”

THE MOMENT OF STILLNESS

"What is stillness?

It is point zero.

The nothingness

Where all that is you, is interconnected with everything around you

It is when magic plays your life, and you play it along....

Have you tried it?

Becoming all that is, when all your inner forces come in together, to create the unpredictable

Let the experience play along

you will be blessed with all its surprises

Trust trust trust"

THE SOUL TRAVELER

“A touch of a heart
with a soul traveler

in simply a perfect body
is a divine creation.

Live your life

& enjoy the perfect world

as it is to learn

grow

& shift things inside out

to see the clear perfection of it!”

SOLITUDE

"**S**eeing

Oneself

Liberated

In-depth

Towards an

Ultimate

Divine

Eternity"

MOMENTS

“Our moments are magical

our energies are contagious

and our life is majestic

Every present is

gracious

elevating

and blossoming.

Let it Be

Forever”

طريق الحق

"الطريق هي رحلة إلى الوجود

فالحياة مليئة بالمغامرات

من

الألغاز والسحر من البداية إلى النهاية

عندما تسير روحك في طريق الحقيقة

جسدك يطير

ويحيا

ويغشى

في الحب"

PATH OF TRUTH

"The path is a journey into being

An adventurous life with so many

mysteries & magic

from a beginning to an end

When your soul walks the path of truth

your body flies

lives

& falls

in Love"

AWAKE IN YOUR SPIRIT

“When the Divine owns your soul

don't be afraid to loose your body

Loose your 'self'

and 'awake' in your spirit”

MARRIAGE RECIPE

“ Marriage recipe;

add a lot of transparency

in communication

with a full sensation of belonging

100% respect

sprinkle daily
the love emotions
and
live in its charm
passion
and
craving ”

♫ LISTEN

"We are abundance

We are love

We are a magnificent creation

We are a bond

A radiating magnet attracting the beautiful powers around you to raw create

it is within

all you need is listen"

TIME

“ We always say:

"You never know when the time is right
but in reality,

it is always the right time" ”

COURAGEOUS

"

Magic, is my description for life

Sparkling, is is how I see life

Courageous, is how I want to live my life!

PRICELESS

"Never count your days as they are too many

Live in its moments as they are

PRICELESS"

UNI-VERSE

"The universe paints our mysterious life
canvas in multiple shapes;

How we perceive it
materializes its exquisiteness and perfection.

Life is simply ours to unfold

Ask for what you desire & it will find you"

LIFE

“ A life can transform in a second

That second belongs to you

Switch
Light up
& Embrace
the power of the universe

You never know what is hiding within you

Believe in it & you'll be created with its energy ”

الكمال

"أعطيتكَ الكمال، فأهملتَ هو

أخذتُ النِصف، ففقدتَ هو

فماذا تراني أفعل، لتلقى هو"

WHOLENESS

"'I' granted you Perfection, & you abandoned 'HU'

'I' extracted the half, & so you astray from 'HU'

What shall I do, so you can encounter 'HU'*"

*Hu or Huwa is a name for God in Sufism
In Arabic: هُوَ meaning "HE"

المرآة الإلهية

" خلقتُ لكَ المياهَ لتعكُس نوري فيها

فنظرتَ الى المياهِ فلم تجد نوري فيها

فلتأخذْ من هذه المياهِ، و لتسقي نفسك فيها

فلعلها تنجلي في اعماقك، فتحلى بنوري فيها "

THE DIVINE'S MIRROR

> "'I' created water, so it mirrors 'My Light.'
>
> You gazed at these waters, & you couldn't perceive 'My Light's reflection
>
> Please grasp these waters, and immerse yourself in 'IT.'
>
> Maybe, 'IT' will wash away your inner struggles
>
> So you submerge yourself with 'My Light.'"

العشق الإلهي

"ما ألهمتُ به،

في العشق

الأعمى يرى

و
الأخرس ينطق

و
الأصم يسمع

و
المُقعد يقف

و
الكل يسجد في حبه"

DIVINE LOVER

“What I channeled,

In Divine Love

The Blind Sees

The Mute Pronounces

The Deaf Hears

The Paralyzed Stands

And

Everyone bows in love”

ॐ

من أنا ، ما أنا ، ما هو الأنا

"أنا، فمن أنا و ما الأنا"
فأرشدني

خلقتكم من روحي و زرعت حباًّ في أنفاسِكم

أبدلتم و أحببتم أنفُسَكم؟

أعطيتكم من خيِّرات الدنيا

أدمّرتم كل معطيات الخير في الدنيا؟

سقيتكم من مياه الحياة و لا خيّرْت من يسقى

فقسَّمتم المياه للأرباح

نسيتم انكم ابنائي و لا أُفرِّق بتاتا

أتفرّقتم و أعطيتم لنفسِكم مقاما؟

ॐ

WHO AM I, WHAT AM I, WHAT IS EGO

“Me, who am I, & what am I?

'HE' Lead me,

I birthed you from my soul and planted love in your breath

You diverted and loved yourselves

'I' gave you the abundance of the world

You've destroyed all the goodness in the world

'I' showered you from the waters of life and didn't choose who immersed in it

So you divided these waters for profit

You forgot you're my children, and I don't make a difference

You split up, and you gave yourselves titles.”

روحي تطير في العشق

فأنا، من أنا؟

فأنا لست بمسلمٍ و لا مسيحيّ، لا يهوديّ و لا
بوذي، و لا ديانةً تعرِّفُ بي

فقد سَكَنتْ روحي هذا الجسد
و استفاقتْ أنفَاسي من هذا الوَرَدْ* و تعلمتْ قِرَّتي
بما أعطاني اياه
الكريم، المحب، الغفور ، الرحوم و الحَيّ

فأصبحتُ إنسان الحياة
و وجَدتُ رحمة العطاء في بِحَارِهِ و بذور محبته و
خدمته في طبيعته

فإعْتَنَقتُ السَلام

فليحيا في قلوبكم كما أُحْيِّيَ في قلبي

* الوَرَدْمن كلمة الأوردة

MY SOUL FLIES IN LOVE

“ I AM. Who am I?

I'm not Muslim, I'm not Christian, I'm not a Jew, I'm not Buddhist, and no religion defines me.

My soul chose this body, and I was awakened in this breath

It is flowing in my veins, and I mastered, through my inner vision, what 'HE' granted me:

the Generous, the Lover, the Forgiver, the Merciful and the Awakener

So I became a being of life

And I found the abundance of giving

in 'HIS' seas,

and the seeds of love and service in 'HIS' nature

And so,

I Embraced Peace
May 'HE" Awaken in your hearts as
'HE' did in mine. ”

خدمة الإنسانية

عندما سألت 'هو

ماذا تراني أفعل لأساعد الناس لتطمئن قلوبهم
فأجابني؛

إعتني بنفسِك

فذهلت

و زاد قائلا

لقد حاولت إرضاء و الإعتناء بكل أبنائي، لتطمئن
القلوب
و الأنفاس

لكن القليلون كانوا حاضرين
اما الاخرون

طريقهم طويلة قبل الوصول

فجلست ساكناً و حمدت 'هو'

SERVING HUMANITY

*When I asked "HIM":

How can I help people flourish with peace in their hearts?

'HE' answered me.

Take care of your SELF.

I was surprised.

'HE' added:

I tried to please and look after all my children, to comfort their hearts and breath,

only a few were present; the others,

they still have a long way to go before they arrive.

So I sat still and gratefully thanked 'HIM.'

WORLD PEACE

“Peace will come upon you, when you become Peace

Love will come upon you, when you become Love

Harmony will come upon you, when you become in harmony with yourself

Forgiveness will come upon you, when you find the ways to forgive yourself and others

The World will be in Peace when you find peace in your Heart”

NOW IS FOREVER

As I fall in the silence of the moment

I dive deep towards the at-one-ment*

Feeling the aliveness of this moment

draws a smile through this attunement**

It is in the now that I can hear the heart beats

& send my gratitude to say thank you for a
hilarious year heat***

Just 4 days to welcome the new, beginning,

Ready for what ever is rising in, my being,

Trust, Love, Faith & Growth
Is all what we have, to dive in this approach
Cheers to what is NOW
As NOW is FOREVER

*At ONE MOMENT: Being ONE with the present
from the word **Attunement: to bring into harmony
Spiritual attunement means hearing God's guidance and aligning our response with it
***Heat, the 2020 year was when I wrote this quote, December 28, 2020, to be precise before entering 2021. Those two years were filled with happenings.

اليقظة

"

الضُّحى هي لحظة اليقظة

و ولادة الحياة في أنفَاسِنا لتشِعَّ في أنفُسِنا روحُنا الطاهرة

فلنُضَحّي في هذه اللحظة

بالأنا' الذي خُلِقَ في الدنيا، و أَبعدَنا عن الحقيقة،

ونقترب من قلوبنا، كي نجد

جزالة كرم الخالق في وجداننا

"

AWAKEN

“The dawn is a moment of awakening

leading to the birth of life through our breath

radiating within us

our pure soul

In this moment

let’s sacrifice the ego that was created in this world

which kept us away from the truth

and let’s come closer to our hearts so we find

the abundance of the Creator in our consciousness”

"EVERYTHING IS POSSIBLE"

This book is simply a glimpse of what has been created in my life. And its main objectives are to inspire you and give you the insight that

"EVERYTHING IS POSSIBLE"

As for my detailed story, per every chapter, you can surely listen to the interviews, podcasts and join me in person at all my conferences and guidance sessions, until another book is born.

AUTHENTIC SMILE

“My smile is contagious

My look is glamorous

and

My passion is desirable

Always charm the universe with your laugh

Your soft vitality

Your high spirit

Your pure honesty

and mostly

Your True Authenticity”

EPILOGUE

Being in a higher state of consciousness is known as a peak experience of awareness when the Divine Being chooses to reveal an aspect of truth about the universal or cosmic reality of existence.

Such experiences are beyond perception of the five senses or rational thinking, they happen instantaneously and are felt by the spiritual heart, they are beyond doubt, we call them insights, inspirations or intuitions of creativity.

They are the source of new discoveries in science, the arts, music, poetry and original new inventions.

Unconditional love is God's most fundamental energy that binds all of existence in wholeness and oneness, this is the divine spirit in manifestation, which is the essence of all that is perceived physically, emotionally, mentally and spiritually.

Reina's book "**When The Divine Speaks The Heart Listens**" is a rare gift of such mystical peak experiences of the sacred spiritual heart feeling the Godhead and universal mind downloading samples of Divine Grace for the good of all.

The new humanity is awakening to the quantum infinite potential that is available to everyone in higher states of awareness to bring love, peace and harmony with compassion as key in all our relationships.

You are an advanced soul having Reina's precious book for your inspiration to participate in making the new golden humanity a reality as you radiate your being of compassion for all.
Enjoy !!!

Fadel Behman, Ph.D, D.Sc
Holistic Energy Physicist

LETTERS & RECOMMENDATIONS

"I had the good fortune over a period of a decade to spend time with Reina at Hippocrates Health Institute, as well as doing retreats with her in Costa Rica. We have had many co-creative conversations over the phone.

This book gives access to Reina's Heart and Soul.

Keep it handy... and in times of stress, a passage will appear that will Empower You toward Peace and Greatness.

I recommend You "gift" this book to Your Family and Your Circle of influence.

It is an Empowering Gift!

Reina truly is an Aquarian Age Pathfinder. Blessings on Your Sacred Journey!

Viktoras Kulvinskas, DD, PhD - co-founder with Dr Ann Wigmore of Hippocrates

Love in Service,
Viktoras Kulvinskas, DD, PhD
Bishop of the Essene Tradition

« Poetic and profound in many ways! Reina's words will touch your heart and soul, and will make you see life in all its beauty.»
Dr. Andreea D. Vanacker - CEO SparkX5

ACKNOWLEDGEMENTS

My Life Transformation and self-discovery journey, have blossomed in this natural way, through the presence of so many angels in my life.

My parents, and my siblings, you are all blessings in my life.

My coaches, guides, and mentors, as well as many of the intangible forces, I am grateful to have you on my path.

My soulful sisters and brothers, we have connected in many levels through out our lives, I am very appreciative of your presence in my life.

The list of gratitude is very long, and you, as a reader, are one of them. I am thankful for YOU.

REINA HALLAB

- Energy Healing Catalyst
- Empowering Public Speaker
- Inspired Writer
- Healthy Vibrant Lifestyle Ambassador
- Personal Development Expert

The time is NOW, EMBRACE YOUR TRUE SELF.

- Plant Based Whole Food - Raw Living Food
- Meditation & Yoga
- Health, Wellness & Well-being
- Environment respect & Sustainability
- Conscious Marketing & Event Producer

A ***passionate***, ***intuitive***, ***caring*** and ***loving being***. She is a ***bundle of energy*** , ***enthusiasm***, ***knowledge*** and ***confidence*** and ***has such a thirst for life.***

Her sensitivity to people's needs and insight into their potential is unmatched. She will guide you towards success in a gentle but determined manner. Reina impresses people with her ***holistic*** approach to mindset. ***She is someone that walks the talk***. She will show you how healthy eating benefits the ***body***, ***mind*** and ***spirit***, as well as is crucial to the welfare of our planet

Connect with Reina through
www.ReinaHallab.com

INFINITE DIVINE LOVE

We all dive in the infinite self
Let there be spaces in your togetherness,
for the Love that flows is Divine

RENA HALLAB
روحٌ حرّة

Printed in the USA
CPSIA information can be obtained
at www.ICGtesting.com
LVHW060810140124
768916LV00041B/1601